# GOTTA GET ME MO

Written by **Kevin Blackmore**,
Buddy Wasisname and the Other Fellers

Illustrations by **Kevin Tobin**

CP
CREATIVE PUBLISHERS
St. John's, NL 2012

Conseil des Arts
du Canada

Canada

We gratefully acknowledge the financial support of the Canada Council for the Arts, the Government of Canada through the Canada Book Fund (CBF), and the Government of Newfoundland and Labrador through the Department of Tourism, Culture and Recreation for our publishing program.



Cover Design and Layout by Kevin Tobin
Illustrations by Kevin Tobin
Printed on acid-free paper

Published by
CREATIVE PUBLISHERS
an imprint of CREATIVE BOOK PUBLISHING
a Transcontinental Inc. associated company
P.O. Box 8660, Stn. A
St. John's, Newfoundland and Labrador A1B 3T7

Printed in Canada by:
TRANSCONTINENTAL INC.

Library and Archives Canada Cataloguing in Publication

Blackmore, Kevin
Gotta get me a moose / written by Kevin Blackmore and Wayne Chaulk, Buddy Wasisname and the Other Fellers ; illustrations by Kevin Tobin.

ISBN 978-1-77103-004-5 (pbk.)

I. Chaulk, Wayne II. Tobin, Kevin, 1958- III. Buddy Wasisname and the Other Fellers IV. Title.

PS8603.L2759G68 2012 C813'.6 C2012-905019-9

Apply for 6 years at $35.00 a crack! Get a Bull Only Licence in an area 300 miles away, and you've got to leave its chummy attached! T'would be a lot easier to read about it than go through it. To you, dear fans, we offer this condensed chronicle as a taste of moose.

– Wayne, Kevin, Ray

To all the great hunters out there, blocked with manly (and womanly) hunting instincts – heave it outta ya! This book is dedicated to you. Please enjoy responsibly.

– KT.

A Wayne Chaulk/Kevin Tobin Production

Written by Kevin Blackmore, Buddy Wasisname and the Other Fellers
Illustrated by Kevin Tobin (KT.)
Art Direction by Mike Barbour

Special thanks to Donna Francis, Pam Dooley and Creative Book Publishing, for all your assistance and support.
And thanks again to Mike Barbour and Gerard Moyst.

## BUDDY WASISNAME AND THE OTHER FELLERS…

In 1983, Ray Johnson, Wayne Chaulk and Kevin Blackmore met. Having spent time playing for enjoyment, the trio found themselves in the summer of '85 playing a ten-day stint at the Newfoundland and Labrador pavilion of Toronto Caravan, a festival celebrating the city's multiculturalism. They were part of an effort that won the Caravan's Best Entertainment award. Things grew until weekends got cluttered doing concerts, and summers were taken up with touring. By 1987, they abandoned all previous occupations and collectively "went at it!" The trio has toured in every province and territory in Canada for more than twenty-seven years.

**Ray Johnson, Job's Cove, Conception Bay, NL**
Sings, plays the accordion and fiddle, assists with the song and recitation writing, contributes a large number of traditional songs, and plays a great straight man in comic routines. Ray is well known as a brilliant instrumentalist.

**Wayne Chaulk, Charlottetown, Bonavista Bay, NL**
Sings, plays the guitar and mandolin, and does a large part of the formal script writing. He does straight man parts as well as characters in the skits. He writes both comic and straight songs and is well known for his contemplative ballads.

**Kevin Blackmore, Glovertown, Bonavista Bay, NL**
Sings, creates noise and acts like a loon with rabies. Contributes to the song and comedy writing and plays guitar, mandolin, bass, banjo and almost anything capable of producing sound if squeezed, shot, banged or broken. He should be contained at all times.

…AND ANOTHER FELLER
**Kevin Tobin (KT.), Conception Bay South, NL**
Can't sing, can't play nothin', but he can draw! Editorial cartoonist for *The Telegram* in St. John's for more than twenty years. Published ten books of his cartoons. *Gotta Get Me Moose, B'y!* is his second illustrated project with Wayne Chaulk and Buddy Wasisname and the Other Fellers.

Like to go moose hunting, hunting in the fall!
Like to go moose hunting, answer the hunting call!
"Gotta get me moose, b'y!"

1,000,000 B.C.

Well first to get a moose licence,
You apply for six whole years.
At 35 dollars a crack, old man,
With a partner for half shares!

MOOSE LICENCE
AREA 28
LICENCE HOLDER:
BUDDY WASISNAME
CO-LICENCE HOLDER:
THE OTHER FELLERS
MAIL

And when you get the licence, cock, tis area 28.
Nowhere near civilization, three hundred miles away!
But "gotta get me moose, b'y!"

Like to go moose hunting, hunting in the fall!
Like to go moose hunting, answer the hunting call!
"Gotta get me moose, b'y!"

AAIEEEEE

To get ya where you're going,
It's a Hilton on four wheels!
Gets easily stuck, and the gas tank leaks
And something up front squeals!

999 A.D.

We met four fellows on a trip, and we got on the beer.
They were on their way to our back yards,
And we was off to theirs! "Gotta get me moose, b'y!"

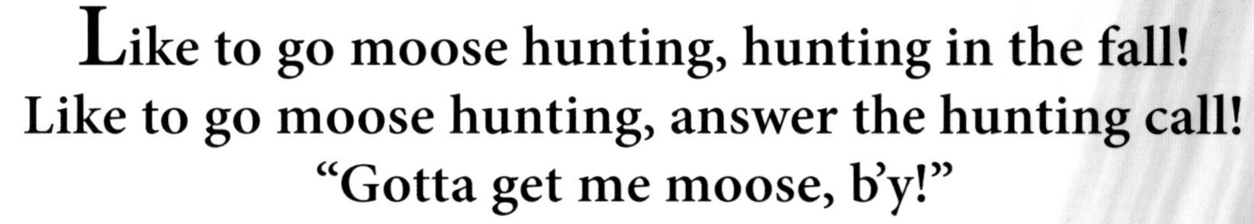

Like to go moose hunting, hunting in the fall!
Like to go moose hunting, answer the hunting call!
"Gotta get me moose, b'y!"

1497

Trottin' on the bogs, me b'ys, with a knapsack on my back.
And you know he's always just ahead,
The fresh buttons in his tracks!

But maybe he can hear us b'ys,
Or maybe it's his snout,
I allow it's not hard to get a whiff of we,
After five or six days out!

WINE
FLOUR
XXX

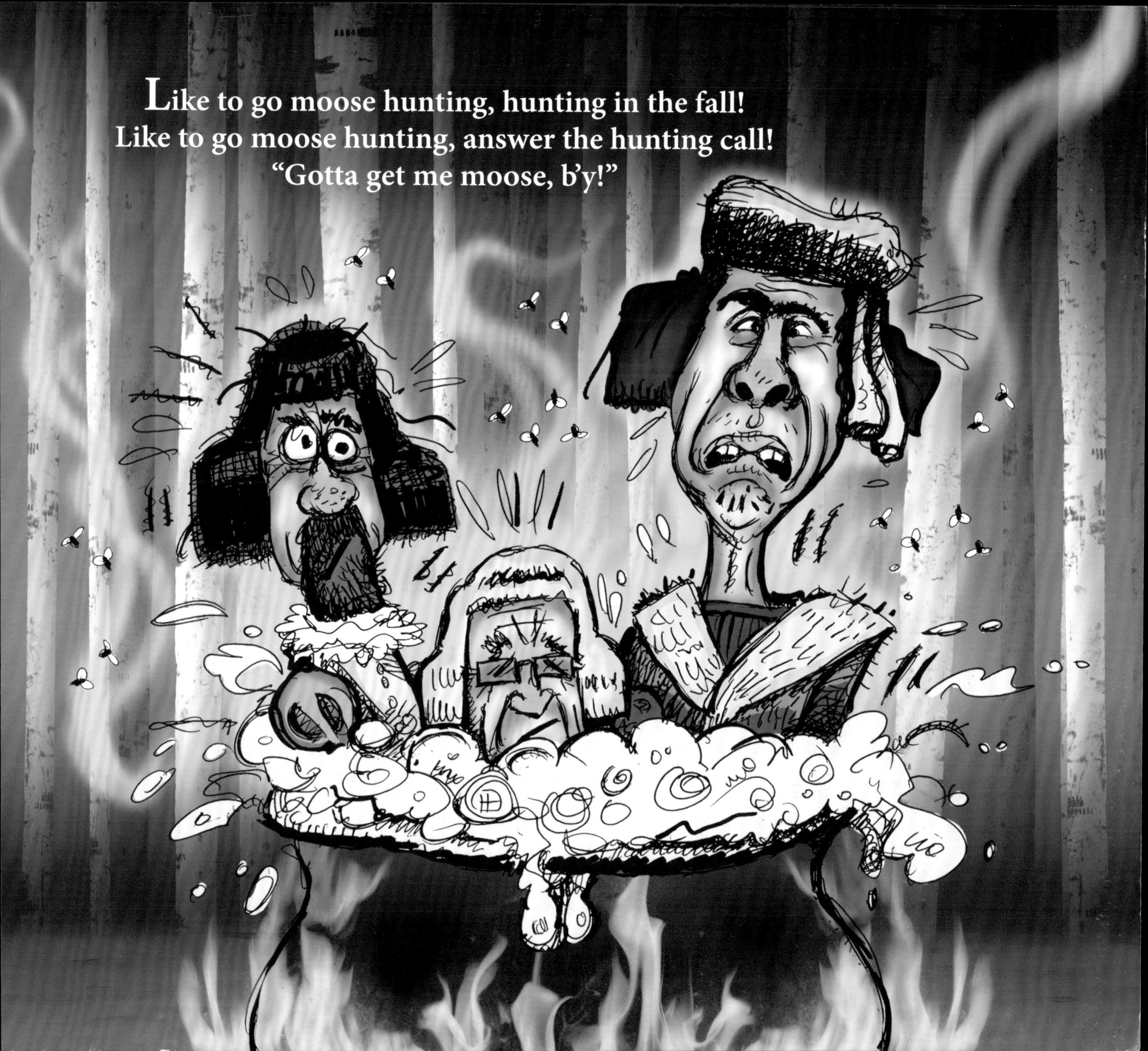
Like to go moose hunting, hunting in the fall!
Like to go moose hunting, answer the hunting call!
“Gotta get me moose, b’y!”

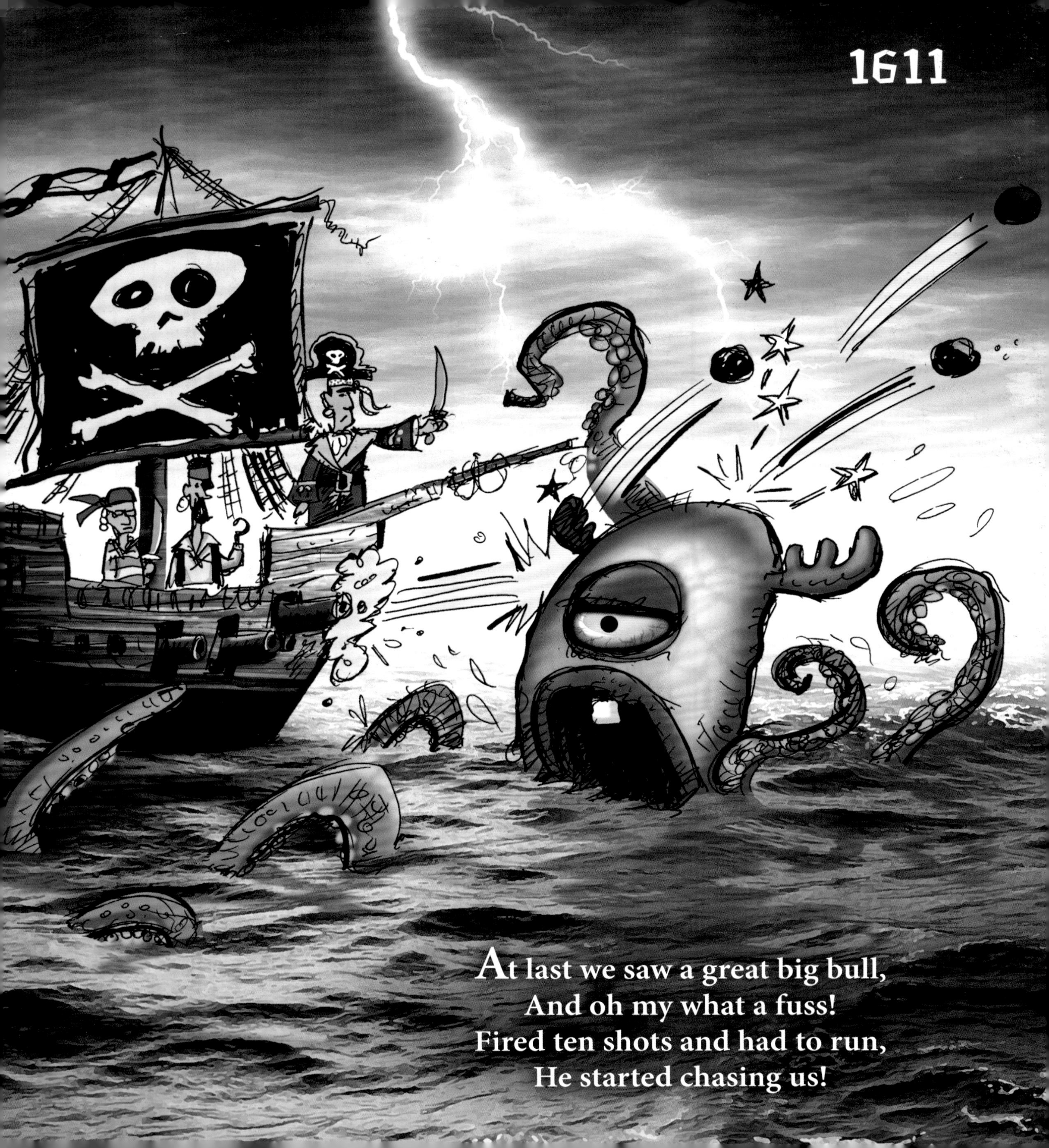


At last we saw a great big bull,
And oh my what a fuss!
Fired ten shots and had to run,
He started chasing us!

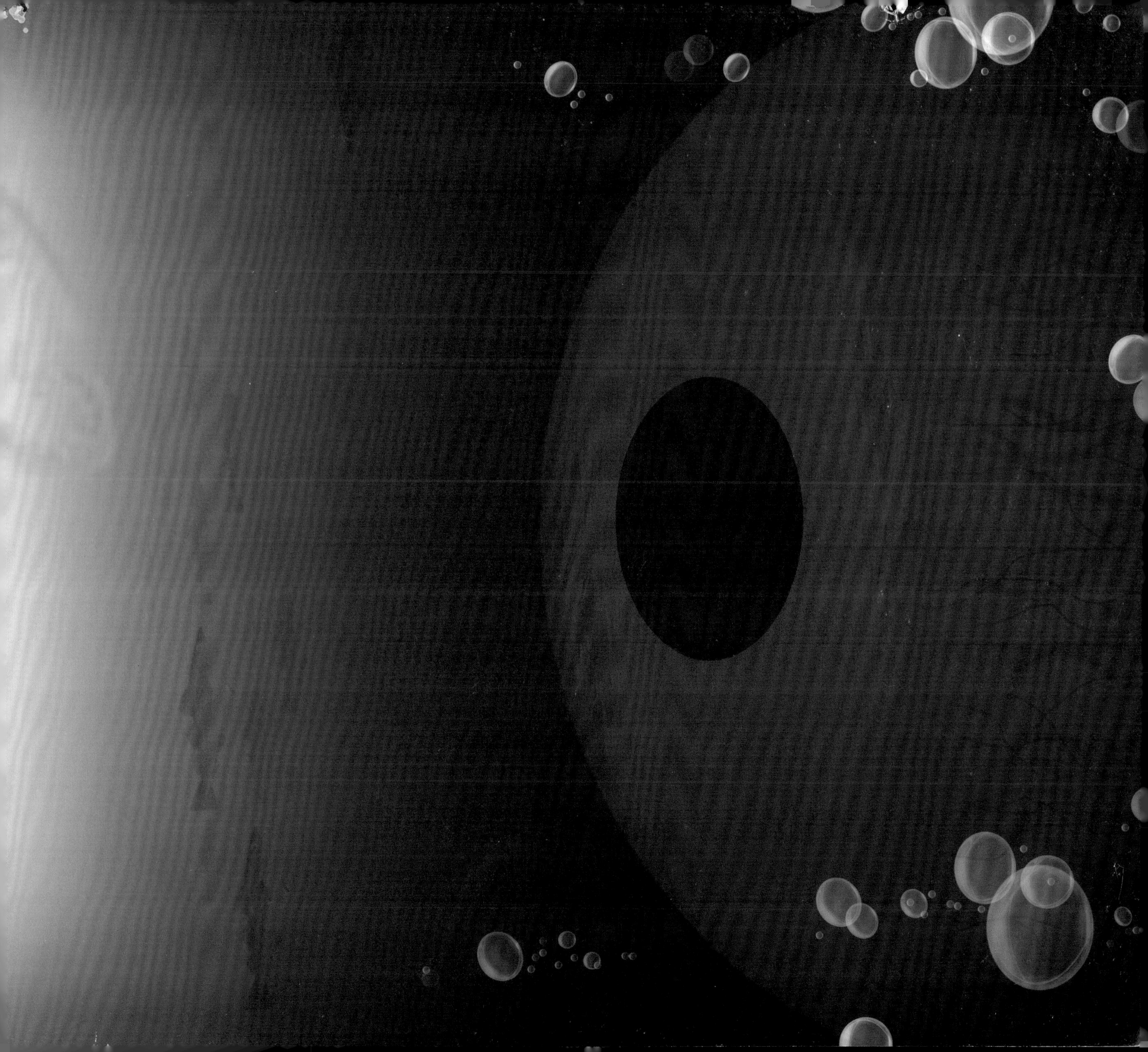

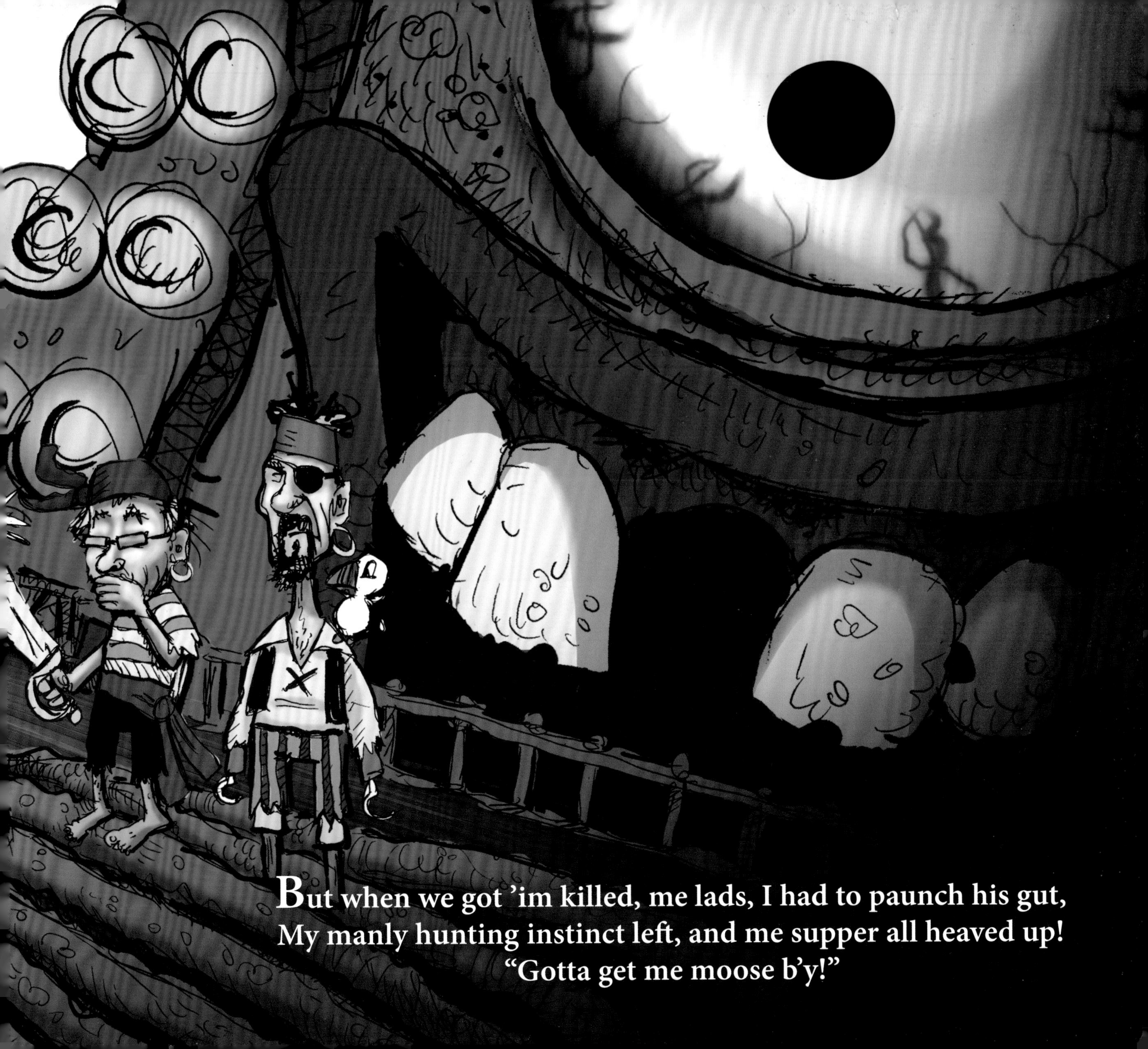

**B**ut when we got 'im killed, me lads, I had to paunch his gut,
My manly hunting instinct left, and me supper all heaved up!
"Gotta get me moose b'y!"

Like to go moose hunting, hunting in the fall!
Like to go moose hunting, answer the hunting call!
"Gotta get me moose, b'y!"

# THIS FALL

Jack, we got to lug him out,
You were nice to have along.
But my next partner will be a wrestler,
Twice as big and strong!

And never again will I go out, across the bog so far,
I wait till I sees one on the road, and I'll wing him with me car! Ha!
That's how I'll get me moose b'ys!

Like to go moose hunting, hunting in the fall!
Like to go moose hunting, answer the hunting call!
"Gotta get me moose, b'y!"

Prior to the release of *Gotta Get Me Moose B'y,* Creative Book Publishing and *The Telegram* partnered to present the contest, "Gotta Get Me Moose *Recipes* B'y," which asked readers to send in their most delicious moose recipe. We have included the top six recipes, as chosen by Buddy Wasisname and the Other Fellers, for your cooking pleasure. Bon appetite!

# Moose Preparation 101

For those of you who are unfamiliar with moose meat, these are a couple things you may find helpful. Moose meat is rich in flavour, lean, and coarse in texture. It can be cooked similar to stewing beef. It may be used as steak and roast, or in soup and stew. When preparing moose as a steak or roast it is favourable to marinate the meat for 24 hours before cooking. This will ensure its tenderness and flavour.

## ISLAND MOOSE STEW – *Joan Whittle, St.John's, NL*

STEW INGREDIENTS:
2-3 lbs. moose steak
2 large onions
1 medium turnip
2 large carrots
1 parsnip
Fat back pork
Salt and pepper to taste

PASTRY INGREDIENTS:
2 cups of flour
3 tsp. baking powder
½ tsp. salt
1 tsp. sugar
Parsley flakes
2 tbsp. butter or margarine
Milk

DIRECTIONS:

1. Fry fat back pork in stew pot until fat is rendered out
2. Season moose with salt and pepper
3. Cut meat in cubes and brown well, with onion
4. Cover with water and simmer until tender (1 ½ - 2 hours)
5. Add cubed vegetables
6. Cook until tender
7. Cover with pastry

PASTRY DIRECTIONS: Place dry ingredients in large bowl. Blend in butter. Add just enough milk to form a soft ball. Pinch off small pieces of dough and shape into patties. Arrange on top of boiling stew. Cover tightly and cook for approx. 10-12 minutes. Thicken stew just before serving.

## BURGUNDY MOOSE – *Dallas Anne Power, Torbay, NL*

INGREDIENTS:
4 lbs. moose cut into bite size pieces
½ cup flour
1 tsp. pepper
1 tsp. salt
3 tbsp. parsley flakes or fresh parsley
⅓ cup vegetable oil
2 large onions, chopped
2 cloves minced garlic
4 cups water
2 beef bouillon cubes
3 bay leaves
2 tsp. lemon juice
2 cans whole mushrooms, undrained
1 ½ cups red wine
¼ cup flour

DIRECTIONS:
1. Combine flour, salt, pepper and parsley, roll moose into flour mixture until evenly coated.
2. In a large Dutch oven, heat oil, add meat and cook until browned. Add onion and garlic.
3. Cook for 5 minutes.
4. Stir in water, bouillon cubes, bay leaves, lemon juice, mushrooms, and 1 cup of wine.
5. Cover and simmer for 2 hours.
6. Just before serving mix together ¼ cup flour and the remaining wine.
7. Stir into simmering liquid, cook until thickened.

## MOOSE CHILI – *Marvin Barnes, St.John's, NL*

INGREDIENTS:

2 lbs. moose (thinly sliced)
½ lb. mushrooms (sliced)
2 onions (chopped)
½ tsp. pepper
2 cans chili beans
1 can of tomato sauce
1 can diced tomatoes
2 bay leaves
3-4 tbsp. chili powder
¼ tsp. crushed chilies
¼ tsp. tabasco
¼ tsp. cayenne pepper
1 tbsp. garlic
Olive oil for frying
1 can or bottle of beer (optional)

Herbs (pinch of each):
Sage
Rosemary
Thyme
Tarragon
Marjoram
Basil

DIRECTIONS:

Sauté onions and mushrooms with pepper. When onions are cooked, add the moose meat and fry until no longer pink. Add herbs, chili powder, cayenne, crushed chilies and garlic. Fry for a further 2-4 minutes.

In a separate pot, combine chili beans, tomato paste, diced tomatoes and bay leaves. Let simmer until it starts to bubble (stir periodically). Add moose meat mixture and simmer for 30 minutes to an hour on low heat. Beer can be added if desired to make chili creamy.

## CURRIED MOOSE – *The Winery Boys, St.John's, NL*

INGREDIENTS:

½ lb. moose roast, cut into chunks.
3 tbsp. olive oil
3 cloves garlic, minced
2 onions, peeled and diced
1 can mushrooms, chopped
2 tbsp. curry powder, or to taste
2 tsp. coriander powder
1 tsp. hot chili powder
1 tsp. ground turmeric
2 carrots, peeled and sliced
1 can of tomatoes
2 potatoes, peeled and cubed
2 cups water

DIRECTIONS:

1. Places all ingredients into roaster and bake at 300°F for 2 hours.
2. Serve on Basmati rice, infused with turmeric, with a side of fresh French bread.

## MOOSE STIR FRY– *Deanne Hiscock, Catalina, NL*

INGREDIENTS:

1 lb. moose steak
2 tbsp. soya sauce.
2 tbsp. brown sugar
1 tsp. oil
1 tbsp. cornstarch
¼ cup pineapple juice
¼ tsp. garlic powder
¼ tsp. ground ginger
1 cup chopped onion
2 tsp. vegetable oil
1 cup sliced red and green pepper
2 cups broccoli, cut into bite sized pieces
½ cup water

DIRECTIONS:

1. Slice meat into thin strips.
2. Combine soya sauce, 1 tsp. oil, cornstarch, brown sugar, pineapple juice, garlic powder, ginger and chopped onion.
3. Add moose meat.
4. Cover and marinate in refrigerator for several hours.
5. In wok or large non stick skillet, stir fry all ingredients until tender.
6. Cover and cook for 3 to 5 minutes or until vegetables are tender crisp.

For variety, try adding celery, carrot, cabbage, cauliflower or mushrooms.

## DRUNKEN MOOSE CREPES – *Denise Browne, Mount Pearl, NL*

INGREDIENTS:

Crepes:

- 1 cup all purpose flour
- 2 eggs
- 1 ¼ cup milk
- 3 tbsp. oil

Marinade:

- 1 lb. moose meat sliced in thin strips
- 1-2 cans of beer enough to cover the moose
- 1 tsp. salt

Filling:

- Cooking Oil
- 2 onions chopped
- Marinated moose meat
- Salt and pepper to taste
- Reserved beer from marinade
- 1 cup of beef broth
- Cornstarch to thicken

DIRECTIONS:

CREPES: In a large bowl, whisk together flour and eggs. Gradually add milk, stirring to combine. Add oil. Whisk until smooth. Cover and set in fridge for about an hour. Heat a lightly oiled frying pan over medium-high heat. Pour or scoop the batter onto the pan, using approximately ¼ cup for each crepe. Tilt the pan with a circular motion so that the batter coats the surface evenly. Pour excess back into the bowl. Cook the crepe for about 2 minutes, until the bottom is lightly brown. Trim off excess to make crepe round. Loosen with a knife or a small baking off-set spatula. Lay them on a cutting board to cool.

DRUNKEN MOOSE: Heat frying pan with cooking oil on medium-high heat. Sauté onions until caramelized. Add marinated moose meat, salt and pepper and fry until brown. Add 1 cup of the beer to the meat and cook until bubbling. When meat is browned, transfer to a roasting pan. Pour the cooked beer into the roaster, clearing the raft first using a sieve. Deglaze the frying pan using the beef broth. Add the broth to the roaster. Cover with aluminum foil making a tight seal and then place the roaster cover over the foil. Place in pre-heated oven of 350°F for 1 ½ hours. Check liquid every ½ hour and add more of the beer/broth, if necessary. Remove from oven and place on stove top on medium-high. Add cornstarch that has been dissolved in water. Stir until sauce is thick.

Place a crepe on a plate. Spoon ¼ cup of the moose mixture onto the centre of the crepe. Fold over the crepe. Spoon some of the sauce over the top of the crepe.